FILL IN THE BLANK BUBBLE WITH **YOUR OWN** INTRODUCTION.

THE D BY NUMBERS

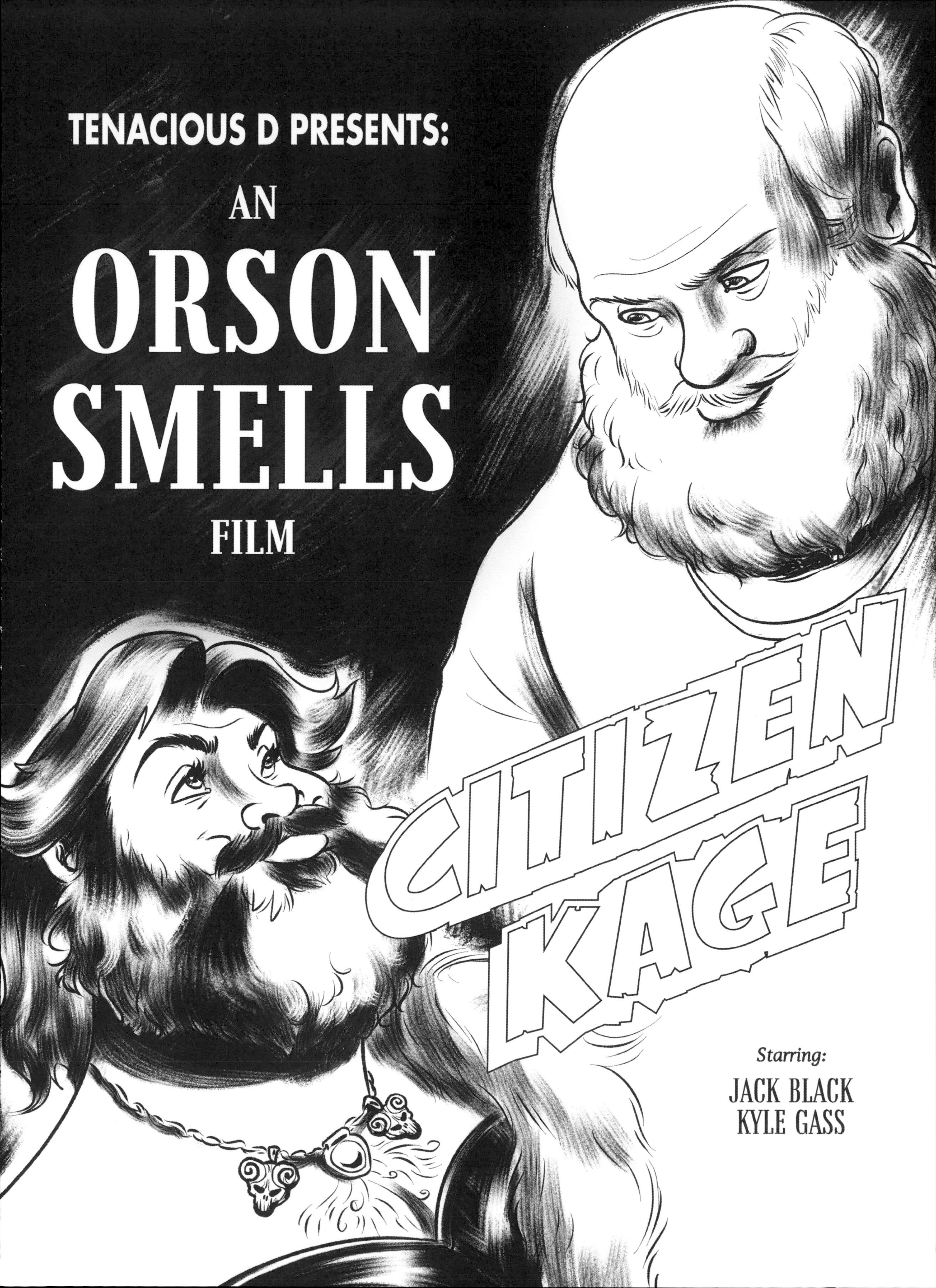

TENACIOUS D PRESENTS:

AN
ORSON
SMELLS
FILM

CITIZEN KAGE

Starring:
JACK BLACK
KYLE GASS

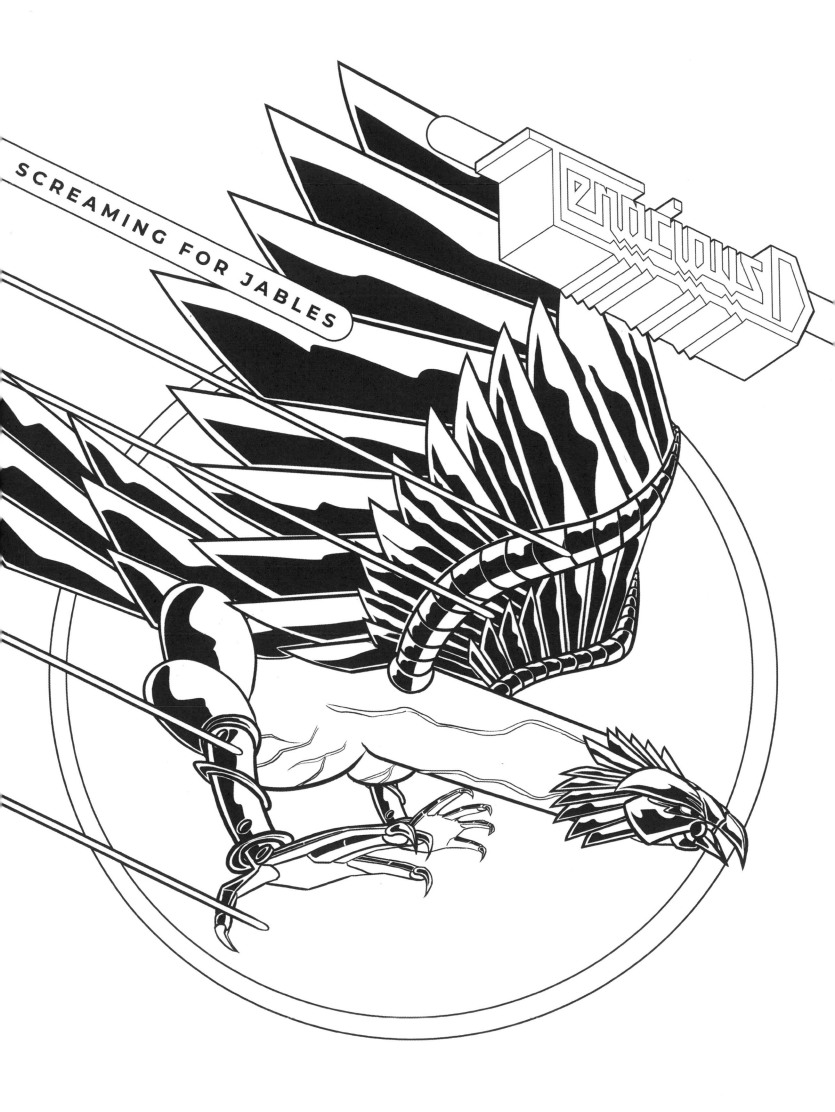

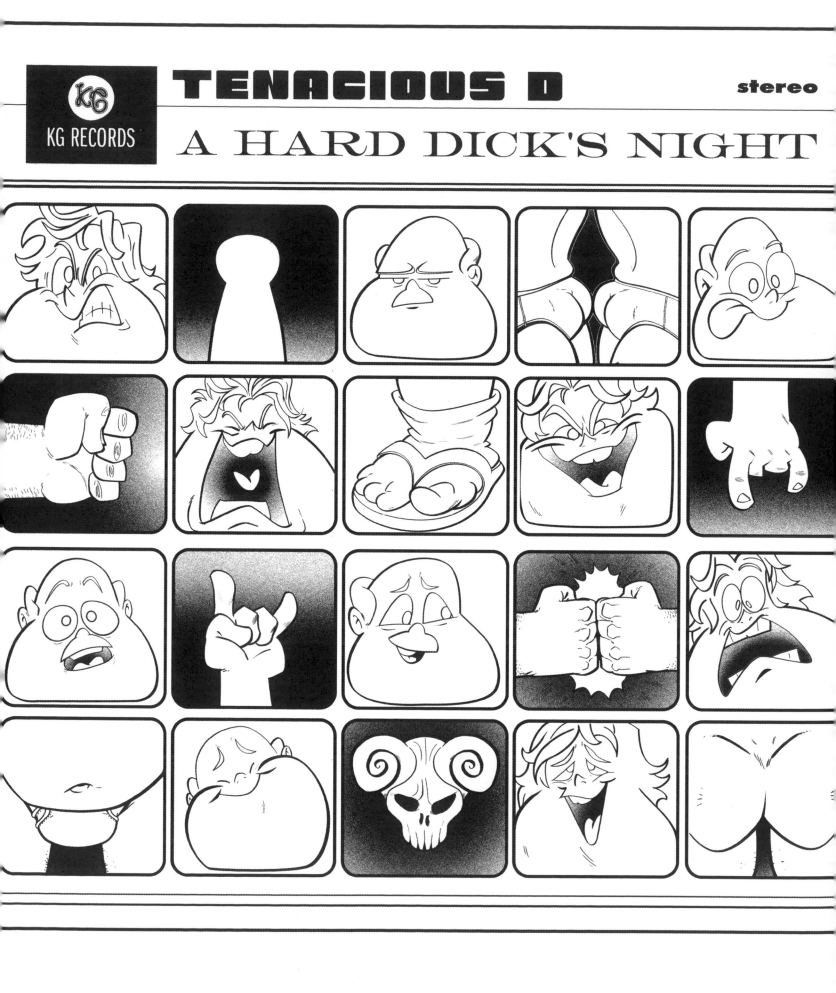

BREAKING NEWS

SEISMIC ACTIVITY IN WESTERN SPRINGS, NEW ZEALAND!

LIVE TD

TENACIOUS D PICTURES PRESENTS:

The Podfather

STARRING

JACK BLACK AND KYLE GASS

AND

JR REED   RONNIE JAMES DIO   MEAT LOAF   TROY GENTILE   BEN STILLER   DAVE GROHL

DIRECTED BY:
LIAM LYNCH

WRITTEN BY:
JACK BLACK, KYLE GASS AND LIAM LYNCH

D NOTE

SIMPLY JAZZ

TD6JB6KG6

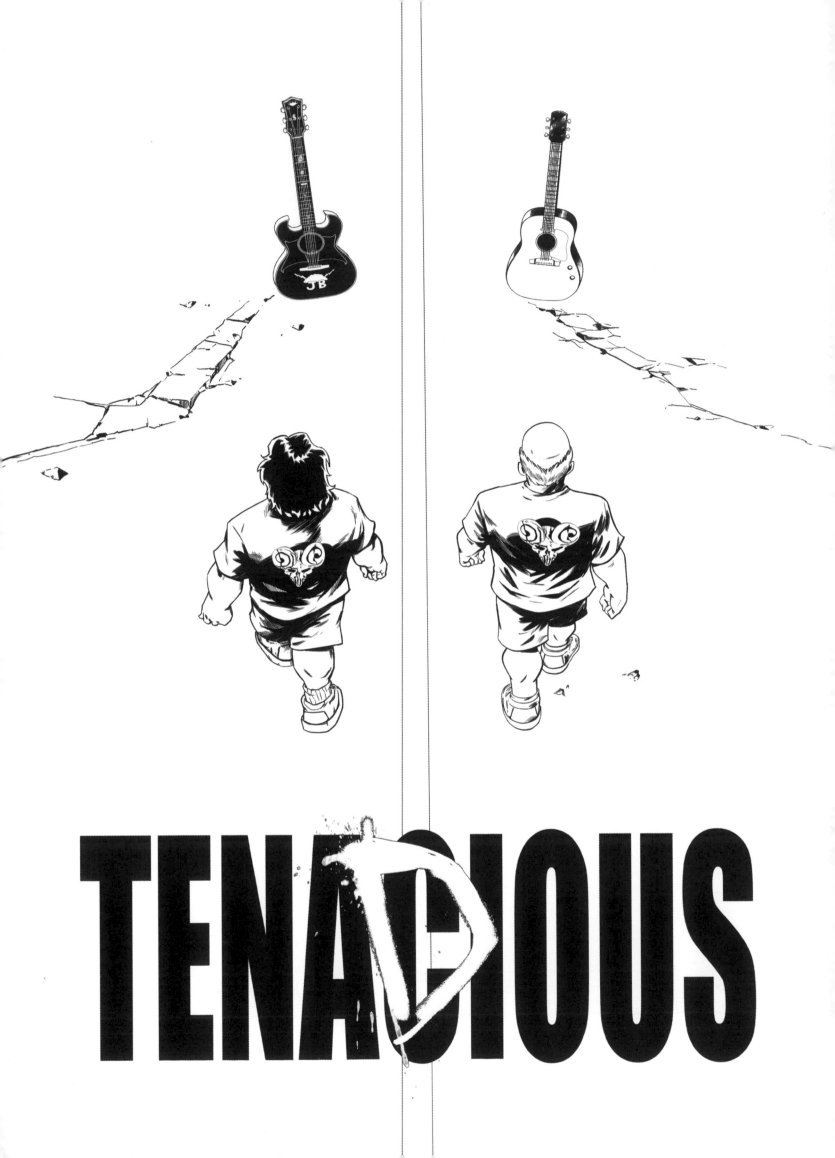

START

END